D0850222

ACCEPTING THE MYSTERY

ACCEPTING THE MYSTERY

Scriptural Reflections for Advent and Christmas

WALTER KASPER

Paulist Press
New York / Mahwah, NJ

Caseside image: Giotto di Bondone (1266–1336), *Nativity*. Photo credit: Alfredo Dagli Orti / Art Resource, NY.
Caseside design by Sharyn Banks
Book design by Lynn Else

Originally published in German in 2015 under the title *Bedenke dein Geheimnis: Meditationen zu Advent und Weihnachten*
Copyright © 2015 by Verlag Katholisches Bibelwerk GmbH: Stuttgart

Translation copyright © 2016 by Paulist Press. Translated by William McDonough.

Library of Congress Control Number: 2016949834

ISBN 978-0-8091-0638-7 (hardcover)
ISBN 978-1-58768-640-5 (e-book)

Published by Paulist Press
997 Macarthur Boulevard
Mahwah, New Jersey 07430

www.paulistpress.com

Printed and bound in the
United States of America

Contents

PART FOUR:
Following the Christmas Star—Epiphany, Baptism of the Lord, and Beyond

Foreword

"Oh, Christian, remember your dignity, and be aware that you share in God's own nature," so does Pope St. Leo the Great (400–461) summarize the Christmas message for us.[1] Against all wishes or temptations to restrict the horizon of human existence to what is feasible, manageable, consumable, the Christian celebration of Christmas gives language to the message of faith: human being, accept the mystery that you are!

And so, in the season of Advent, the church reflects both on biblical texts of repentance and judgment, and on the mystery of grace. Because of God's victorious grace we can take up the Christmas message of the angel that night at Bethlehem, and we can follow the star that leads us to worship the Son of God. This book brings together homilies I have given over the years in the Advent and Christmas seasons. I have revised and brought them together in this volume with the wish and desire that they may help strengthen readers' hope, faith, and trust that the future belongs to that child in the manger.

---

1. Sermon 21: 3. St. Leo preached this sermon on Christmas Day in the year 440. A good English translation can be found in St. Leo the Great, *Sermons* (*Fathers of the Church Patristic Series*, vol. 93), trans. Jane Patricia Freeland, C.S.J.B. and Agnes Josephine Conway, S.S.J. (Washington, DC: The Catholic University of America Press, 1996), 79.

I am very grateful to Dr. Ulrich Sander for his careful work of editing this book and for his translation of some of the texts cited here.

Cardinal Walter Kasper
Feast of the Transfiguration of the Lord
(August 6, 2015)
Wangen im Allgäu, Germany

PART ONE

MEETING THE LORD— ENTERING ADVENT

Judgment and Grace

In those days, the crowds asked John the Baptist, "What then should we do?" In reply he said to them, "Whoever has two coats must share with anyone who has none; and whoever has food must do likewise." Even tax collectors came to be baptized, and they asked him, "Teacher, what should we do?" He said to them, "Collect no more than the amount prescribed for you." Soldiers asked him, "And we, what should we do?" He said to them, "Do not extort money from anyone by threats or false accusation, and be satisfied with your wages."

As the people were filled with expectation, and all were questioning in their hearts concerning John, whether he might be the Messiah, John answered all of them by saying, "I baptize you with water but one who is more powerful than I is coming; I am not worthy to untie the thong of his sandals. He will baptize you with the Holy Spirit and fire. His winnowing fork is in his hand, to clear his threshing floor and to gather the wheat into his granary; but the chaff he will burn with unquenchable fire. So, with many other exhortations, he proclaimed the good news to the people." (Luke 3:10–18—Gospel for the Third Sunday of Advent, Lectionary Cycle C)

John the Baptist is a great Advent figure pointing to the coming of the Messiah. He compares the coming Christ to a farmer holding a spade in his hand, ready to separate the wheat from the chaff and burn the chaff in the fire.

There are many who think as follows: this not only does not fit in our time; it also does not fit in the gospel. Is the gospel not good news, intended to bring comfort and joy, freeing us from anxiety and terror? Does not the gospel say that there is hope for every human being, that God accepts and affirms every human being? How do such threats fit with all that?

Many today simply omit the message of judgment; they suppress and forget it. If that is the case, we must simply leave out many chapters of the Bible, whether from the prophets of the Old Testament or from the preaching of Jesus himself. The prophets are especially harsh in their critique of false prophets who flatter their listeners and radiate confidence without speaking of judgment.

With false prophets there is no time of reckoning. People need not let themselves be addressed by the judging word of true prophets, of the Baptist, and of Jesus himself. But this is a key part of the Sacred Scriptures. We must take it seriously and ask ourselves what God wants to say to us through this Word.

I want to be specific here at the beginning and present a thesis that, at first glance, seems paradoxical. But here it is: the message of judgment is itself a message of grace.

Whoever does not take the word of judgment seriously and thinks it can simply be ignored also does not take grace seriously. Such a person turns grace into "cheap grace" and trivializes Christianity.

Whoever only knows the saccharine "dear God"—a God so loving as to say only "yes" and "amen" to everything—at base has not understood anything about God. In fact, in the end, such a person does not have any God at all, but only a made up and projected image of his own happiness and blissful fantasies. For it belongs to God who is good to stand against evil: God hates injustice, violence, and lies and wants to eliminate them.

God does not want all the terrible wrong and blatant injustice, the murders, the destruction, the desecration. God's anger and wrath are enkindled against them. In the end, what God wants is that the murderer not triumph over his victim, that no one get away with lies and deceit, that injustice not win the day, that it is not only the rights of the strong that count, and that evil not have a future. What God works for is that in the end all are truly equal, that all masks fall away and that the truth comes to light. God's desire is that truth instead of lies, that justice instead of power, and that love instead of hate triumph in the end.

Can we even think of a meaningful world without the triumph of the good and the true? Would we not have to give up all hope of meaning without such a final judgment? And isn't this judgment precisely a hope for the poor and insignificant, for those who have no voice in the world with which to defend themselves?

If this were not so, then history would be judge of the world; and history would be simply a history of the winners, where in the end victims, the oppressed, the murdered, and the desecrated go away empty-handed and the good are left without voice.

And so must we not say that it is truly grace that God turns out to be the judge and has the last word? Therefore, the message of judgment is also a message of grace; the message of judgment is a message of hope.

John the Baptist goes yet another step further. He does not only tell us what God is like and what God does; he tells us what we who hear his message should do. He calls us to repent and reform our lives. Certainly, there is a great temptation to think: "Yes, others should and must change their lives, but for the most part I'm OK. I can admit to small errors, but I surely don't belong among the great sinners."

That may even be true. But is it enough? For John the Baptist and for Jesus it is clearly not enough. Their message calls out to us to take the side of goodness, of justice, and of truth—just as God does. It is not enough to avoid evil; what we must do is stand up for goodness.

This becomes clear in John's first response to the question: What must we do? He replies: "Whoever has two coats, let him share with whoever has none; whoever has food should do likewise." To repent means to decide for these alternatives and to live according to them. Just as God is a God of hope, so should we also be signs of hope in the world. We should be witnesses to a new world, witnesses to the choice for truth, for justice, and for love. We should show that it can be different and that this is the better way. In doing so, we will bring hope to many.

When we judge others critically and mercilessly, we witness against hope and not for it. We are not judges; only God can judge what is within human beings. We are not judges, but are to be like doctors: we are to heal wounds suffered on account of evil; we are to do the good we can do. One good deed is more valuable than a thousand moral sermons. As Augustine put it, we are to hate evil but love evildoers. For God does not want the death of the sinner, but that he should repent and live.

In the forward to his book *Discipleship*, the Protestant pastor and theologian Dietrich Bonhoeffer (1906–1945) wrote the following:

> Today it seems so difficult to walk with certainty the narrow path of the church's decision and yet to remain wide open to Christ's love for all people, and

in God's patience, mercy and loving-kindness (Titus 3:4) for the weak and godless. Still, both must remain together, or else we will follow merely human paths. May God grant us joy in all seriousness of discipleship, affirmation of sinners in all rejection of sin, and the overpowering and winning word of the gospel in all defense against our enemies.[1]

In his book written in the middle of the last century's persecution, this great witness of faith warned against cheap grace, against being a Christian without repentance and penance, without the fruits of the Spirit. Again today there is a danger of a polite, bourgeois Christianity that barely distinguishes itself from the world as it is.

John speaks of a baptism by fire; he also promises a baptism in the Holy Spirit. For us, it means that we need to live from the fire of the Holy Spirit, becoming fiery Christians driven by God's Holy Spirit: "For everyone will be salted with fire" (Mark 9:49).

---

1. Bonhoeffer wrote these words in 1935–36, and his book was published in Germany in 1937. The English translation here is by Barbara Green and Reinhard Krauss, as found in: Geoffrey B. Kelly and John D. Godsey, editors, Dietrich Bonhoeffer, *Discipleship, Dietrich Bonhoeffer Works, Volume 4* (Minneapolis, MN: Fortress Press, 2001), 40. The editors explain: "The 'church's decision' refers specifically to the Confessing Church and its decision to resist incorporation into the [Third] Reich Church." Ibid.

Where We Can Place Our Trust

Jesus said to his disciples, "But in those days, after the suffering, the sun will be darkened, and the moon will not give its light, and the stars will be falling from heaven, and the powers in the heavens will be shaken. Then they will see the Son of Man coming in the clouds with great power and glory. Then he will send out the angels, and gather his elect from the four winds, from the ends of the earth to the ends of heaven.

"From the fig tree learn its lesson: as soon as its branch becomes tender and puts forth its leaves, you know that summer is near. So also, when you see these things taking place, you know that he is near, at the very gates. Truly I tell you, this generation will not pass away until all these things have taken place. Heaven and earth will pass away, but my words will not pass away.

"But about that day or hour no one knows, neither the angels in heaven, nor the Son, but only the Father. Be aware, keep alert, for you do not know when the time will come. It is like a man going on a journey, when he leaves home and puts his servants in charge, each with his work, and commands the doorkeeper to be on the watch. Therefore, keep awake—for you do not know when the master of the house will come, in the evening, or at midnight, or at cockcrow, or at dawn, or else he may find you asleep when he comes suddenly. And what I say to you I say to all: Keep awake." (Mark 13:24–37—Gospel for the First Sunday of Advent, Lectionary Cycle B)

We live in unsettling times: times full of bloody conflicts, of malicious terrorist attacks, of insecurity and fear of what may come next. Accepted values and order have been shaken; many people have become disoriented. For many the only things that still matter are material goods and immediate private advantage.

For us Christians, Advent serves as a break each year, a time to stop and reflect again on what sustains and supports us and on what gives our lives meaning and direction.

Among the biblical texts that are read in the Advent prayer of the church are apocalyptic visions of the "end of the world." The thirteenth chapter of the Gospel of Mark paints a picture of terrors: the sun and the moon will be darkened, stars will fall out of the skies, and the powers of the heavens will be shaken.

These images come out of a bygone worldview, but even today they have something decisive to say to us: our world will not last forever, and nothing in this world is eternal. The apparently secure orders, those to which we most entrust ourselves, are fleeting. One day the great system of this world and the great systems that belong to this world will all break down. In the end, one cannot rely on them.

Haven't we ourselves often experienced this? Of the mighty empires of history, of their fabulous wealth and their cities filled with art and treasures, only ruins remain. In recent history, the

Berlin Wall and the Iron Curtain have fallen and, along with them, the Soviet empire which strove for world domination and the ideology of communism collapsed almost overnight.

Yes, what the apostle Paul said is true: "The present form of this world is passing away" (1 Cor 7:31). Whoever relies on it builds his life on the shifting sands of history which the winds of time blow away. "You fool!," says Jesus. "This very night your life is being demanded of you" (Luke 12:20).

Yet the thirteenth chapter of the Gospel of Mark does not end with a message of terror. Much more, it tells us what remains, where we can place our trust, and what is lasting upon which we can build our lives: "Heaven and earth will pass away, but my words will not pass away" (Mark 13:31). For God is trustworthy; we can rely on God. We can build on God's Word: "You, O LORD, are our father; our Redeemer from of old is your name" (Isa 63:16).

Above all, the Word of God is a Word of promise and of hope. It says to us: God is the Lord of the world and of history. God holds all things in his hands. In the end, God will gather the scattered elect, those made righteous by God's grace, those who lived according to his Word; from all the ends of the earth God will gather them and raise up the kingdom of peace, justice, truth, and love. And God will be all in all (1 Cor 15:28).

And so God's commandments also have lasting value. They are not obsolete old-fashioned leftovers, but are still a reliable pathway for us now. They do not aim to constrict our lives or take away our freedom. They are words of life, seeking to help us so that our lives will be successful and happy; they seek to lead us to true life, fulfilled life, eternal life.

In our times, when many people are disappointed by life and when hope is in short supply, when disappointment, discouragement, and resignation prevail, we can be people of Advent, people of trust, witnesses to hope. For no one can live without hope: no person, no nation, and above all not the church. We should testify to the truth that life and the world do not come to nothing, but open into the kingdom of God.

What follows from this? Not a carefree light-heartedness that thinks that things aren't so bad, that nothing is that important and everything will all turn out OK in the end. Such a superficial "happy ending" stance is completely foreign to the gospel of Jesus; he speaks a different, much more serious language: "Be aware, and keep alert!"

So that we too will take this call seriously, Jesus repeats a second time: "Be aware, keep alert." That means do not fall asleep or be lulled into a false sense of security! "For you do not know when the time will come."

Christian hope is not aimed at "pie in the sky by and by." It is no remote utopian dream. Hope in the coming of Christ is aimed at this moment: now is the time; now is the hour. Every day counts. Every moment can be God's time.

That is what is being said to us today. Sluggishness, care-lessness, and sleepiness are a great danger for us Christians. And so it says in the New Testament: "Keep alert. Like a roaring lion your adversary the devil prowls around, looking for someone to devour" (1 Pet 5:8). The fight against evil, against temptation must continue each day.

Every day is the time for Christians to be alert and recognize the "signs of the times," to grasp opportunities that open up to them, and to do whatever is possible that day with prudence but also with courage and confidence. Advent should take place in the midst of everyday life in this world, for God wants to enter into us through a life of prayer and the works of love.

In faith we know this: Jesus Christ, the Lord of the church, is with us always, to the end of the earth (Matt 28:20). This trust and this hope are vital for our whole existence as Christians. As Advent people, we do not build on the structures of this world; we are much more filled with hope in the coming world. And so every day we can carry the share of the load that is expected of us with courage, and we can become ready every day anew for God and his kingdom, that is, for righteousness and peace and joy in the Holy Spirit (Rom 14:17).

PART TWO

THE MESSAGE OF NAZARETH— KEEPING ADVENT WITH MARY

In the sixth month the angel Gabriel was sent by God to a town in Galilee called Nazareth, to a virgin engaged to a man whose name was Joseph, of the house of David. The virgin's name was Mary. And he came to her and said, "Greetings, favored one! The Lord is with you." But she was much perplexed by his words and pondered what sort of greeting this might be. The angel said to her, "Do not be afraid, Mary, for you have found favor with God. And now, you will conceive in your womb and bear a son, and you will name him Jesus. He will be great and will be called the Son of the Most High and the Lord God will give to him the throne of his ancestor David. He will reign over the house of Jacob forever, and of his kingdom there will be no end." Mary said to the angel, "How can this be, since I am a virgin?" The angel said to her, "The Holy Spirit will come upon you, and the power of the Most High will overshadow you; therefore the child to be born will be holy; he will be called Son of God. And now, your relative Elizabeth in her old age has also conceived a son; and this is the sixth month for her who was said to be barren. For nothing will be impossible with God." Then Mary said, "Here am I, the servant of the Lord; let it be with me according to your word." Then the angel departed from her. (Luke 1:26–38—Gospel for the Fourth Sunday of Advent, Lectionary Cycle B)

Light from Nazareth

Luke's story of the Annunciation of the angel Gabriel to Mary is familiar to us, perhaps too familiar. But we must not rush through this story; for it is not just any reading from the Bible, but the gospel announcing salvation to us and the whole world. It is the gospel of the Messiah, the Savior of the world. This is good news for all of us. It says that neither this world of ours, so often full of evil, despair, suffering, and death, nor our own lives are forgotten or lost. A light shines on us from a small house in Nazareth, a light that, like the morning star shining in the darkness of night, heralds the rising of the sun and the beginning of a new day.

A young woman is destined to be the mother of the Most High, mother of God's own Son, who will come to bring the kingdom of God, a kingdom of justice and peace, of mercy and love, a kingdom that will carry the day over the kingdoms of this world and maintain its rule forever.

Yes, God himself will come and have the final word, wiping away all tears and fulfilling all prayers, all longings, all hopes.

This is no mere pipe dream, no utopia. It became reality because this young woman Mary—in spite of her questions, uncertainty, and doubt—gathered all her courage and said: "Yes; here I am, the servant of the Lord." And so she became the dawn preceding the sunrise of salvation, the Mother of Good Hope who gives strength and radiance to the hope in our own lives.

This story in Luke's Gospel deals with the dawn of and the opening to our salvation, the salvation of the whole world. What happened to the Virgin Mary also happens to us; she said her "yes" to God's call, gave her response to the angel, as our representative and our example. And so she became the model for every Christian and for the whole church.

Perhaps one or another person will think as follows: I have never had the experience of an angel being sent to me. It is true enough that what happened to Mary was extraordinary and unique. But it was not unique in the sense that would keep us from saying in an analogous and figurative way that what happened to Mary does indeed happen to us. We must not remain in a quasi-naturalistic or miraculous understanding of what Luke describes with the appearance of the angel. God can speak to us in many different ways and can send us an angel without the wings we imagine; who instead has two legs, two hands, and a mouth and through whom a message reaches us (perhaps completely unknown to its sender), a message that finds an echo in our hearts.

As I see and understand her, Mary was a person who quieted herself and listened, a person who listened with and within her heart as God spoke to her about what God wanted from her and about what her life's task would be; we, on the other hand, are too often focused on the outside world, distracted by many things that seem important or interesting and fascinating. Because we are like this, we miss or crowd out the voices that speak to us from the depths and in silence. And so we have to ask ourselves: Are we really aware of what is happening to us in our own depths, of what God is saying to us, of what God wants from us? The season of Advent is an invitation to take some distance and learn to listen.

If we do so, it may happen that in the silence we too will hear an *"Ave,"* our own "Hail, blest are you." Each of us will become aware that we have a name: my own personal name, which distinguishes me from everyone else. We will be aware that this name is not simply the one by which we are called by family and friends, but the name by which God is calling us. God knows me; God has called me from before time and will never forget me. That I am here is not the result of blind coincidence or the product of an undirected evolution. On the contrary, I am here as a person who deserves to be greeted, who deserves a welcome in this world: "The Lord is with you." Grace reigns and holds sway over my life. The following words apply to me as they do to all human beings: "Do not be afraid, for you have found favor with God."

This insight makes us aware of something more. Yes, God wants me to exist and loves me, but God also wants something from me. I have a task, a mission in this world. It is not exactly the same as Mary's mission of being God's mother. But we, too, every single one of us, have the task and mission of receiving God in our own hearts—not as a gift for ourselves and not as our private property—but as a gift, a present for others. A light should also go out from us, a light that makes the darkness of the world just a little brighter; we too are to be signs of hope.

Certainly, questions and doubts arise immediately: How can that happen? And the answer to this question is the same as the answer that Mary received: the Holy Spirit will come upon you, the Spirit of counsel and strength, of wisdom and of courage. But God's Spirit does not take ahold of us without our help; the Spirit awaits our answer, our readiness, our "yes."

The story that began in the small house in Nazareth continues on. It finds its continuation through all the centuries in the lives of holy women and men who have carried the torch further, and from whom the world receives light. Today it is our own task to become small morning stars, announcing the sun of justice and love through our witness to Jesus Christ our Savior.

The Power of Grace

"Do not be afraid, Mary, for you have found favor with God" (Luke 1:30). As the one who found favor with God, the graced one, Mary accomplishes nothing on her own. She owes all that she is and does to the grace that God has given through Jesus Christ, grace at work in her to prepare her to become the mother of God. Mary does not displace or eclipse Christ in any way. On the contrary, in the beauty of who she is, Mary shows how the grace of Christ works and becomes fruitful.

In this sense and over time, the church has increasingly understood the words "full of grace" in such a way that Mary is seen as having been "full of grace" from the beginning and in every dimension of her being. From the very beginning there was no taint of sin, of evil, of being lost in her. And so she was the purest and most perfect creature of God's grace. As such, as the mother of God, she was to be both a dwelling place for and the entryway of God into the world.

So Mary is the sign that, despite all sin and evil, God has not abandoned the world and humanity but has continued to support us. God has in effect preserved a place of healing, an intact person, a place of safety from which God could begin to reclaim us human beings and bring us home into his kingdom.

Mary reminds us of something that we are in danger of

forgetting in our widely secularized world: the primacy of grace. We do not live from ourselves, but from grace. Everything that we have and are is a gift. In the end, what counts is God's grace—not what we "make." It may still look bleak in the world, and evil may still appear so powerful. Yet everything is enveloped by an even greater grace.

And so these words also apply to us: "Do not be afraid, for you have found favor with God." They are especially important words for us today. For fear is all around us. We live in a time of great upheaval in all spheres of life. Much that is foundational is changing. We have many questions: Where can we place our hope? What can we rely upon? What can we hold on to, and what will sustain us?

The answer rings out: "Do not be afraid, for you have found favor with God." Have no fear! Grace, the primal benevolence, wants to say to us, There is one who wishes you well. This "one" is not just anybody. It is God, the deepest mystery and the Lord of all reality. God's favor is turned toward you. God holds and sustains you. God loves you, has chosen you from eternity and has—as the prophet Isaiah (49:16) puts it—carved you in the palm of his hand. God never ever forgets you. Even more: God is not only near you and with you; God is in you. God shares himself with you and gives himself to you. God lives in you and in your heart. You are a temple of the Holy Spirit. God "has blessed us in Christ with every spiritual blessing in the heavenly places, just as he chose us in Christ before the foundation of the world to be holy and blameless before him in love. He destined us for adoption as his children through Jesus Christ, according to the good pleasure of his will, to the praise of his glorious grace that he freely bestowed on us in the Beloved" (Eph 1:3–6).

The "yes" that God spoke to Mary enabled her to proclaim her own full and undivided "yes" to God and God's will. In the power of God's "yes," she herself said "yes": "I am the servant of the Lord; let it be with me according to your word."

This *fiat*, "so be it," was not easy for Mary. From the beginning, she did not understand how this was to happen. And later she had to persevere in her "yes." Already when Jesus was twelve she had to search for him for three days with great worry before finding him in the temple. And when Jesus began his public ministry, her own questions arose; she wanted to bring Jesus back home. And, in the end, she had to follow her Son right up to the cross. We sing the *Stabat Mater*: She stood, she remained steadfast and stable even under the cross.[1] She stood by her "yes," faithful even in pain. Like us, she traveled the pilgrim way of faith. She is our sister in faith.

And so Mary is teacher and model for our discipleship, for our Christian life. Mary, our sister and companion on the pilgrim way of faith, says to us what she said at the marriage feast in Cana of Galilee: "Do whatever he [Christ] tells you" (John 2:5). She shows us what is important: to do God's will and dedicate ourselves to becoming holy. "Just as he chose us in Christ before the foundation of the world to be holy and blameless before him in love" (Eph 1:4).

This does not entail doing extraordinary things, but doing ordinary things with extraordinary fidelity. As the fully favored and holy one, Mary has shown us the way inward and upward.

---

1. The *Stabat Mater* ("the mother stood") is a thirteenth-century Catholic hymn to Mary, which portrays her suffering as Jesus Christ's mother during his crucifixion. As a common English translation has it: "At the cross her station keeping, stood the mournful mother weeping…"

The Prince of Peace

The Annunciation of the angel to Mary takes up the promises of the prophets and the yearning hope of Israel and of all humanity. The angel heralds the hoped-for Messiah, to whom the Lord God will give the throne of David and whose kingdom will have no end. He is the Prince of Peace (Isa 9:6). These are powerful images. They radiate the kind of hope against hope that we urgently need in our own situation, for there is a significant shortage of hope in our world. These images can encourage us. For such hope thwarts our obsessive and seemingly inevitable conflicts. It says to us: In God's eyes, the world is not really as it sometimes seems from our human perspective. From God's perspective a saving way out is possible.

But, how? Precisely this is Mary's question. She asks, "How can this be?" How can it be that Mary, a virgin, should expect a child, the longed-for Messiah? From a human perspective this is impossible, out-of-touch wishful thinking, perhaps even a delusion. But Mary receives an answer: "Nothing is impossible for God. The Holy Spirit will come upon you, and the power of the Most High will overshadow you." That is the answer. Through the wonderful work of the Spirit—the miracle of Christmas—the coming of the Savior and the beginning of a new world becomes possible.

The divine breath of life, called Holy Spirit in the Bible, is at work in all living things; it is the creative power of God that, through all afflictions and catastrophes, leads the world and history toward their fulfillment in the messianic kingdom of peace, of freedom, of justice, of life, and of love. It is not a spirit of force that compels from the outside; it is the Spirit that works from within, that stirs in the human heart and conscience, implanting hope, giving patience and courage, bringing imagination and insight, to withstand and overcome difficulties, in order to transform the world from within and instill at least a reflection of Christmas peace.

Peace in the world starts small: in the heart and in thoughts of peace, in the everyday lives of each of us, in families and in workplaces, in neighborhoods, and in many individual human encounters. From there it streams out into the larger world of politics. Peace also began in a very small way at Christmas: in a small, weak, defenseless child. And yet the light emanating from the manger of Bethlehem has lost none of its fascination up to our own day. God reveals his power and greatness in weakness. If we confess our faith in this child as the Prince of Peace, the One whose dominion is without end, then we must change our thinking, renounce violence, and become peacemakers through many small acts of love.

PART THREE

CELEBRATING CHRISTMAS

Christ, the Savior, Is Born

In those days a decree went out from Emperor Augustus that all the world should be registered. This was the first registration and was taken while Quirinius was governor of Syria. All went to their own towns to be registered. Joseph also went from the town of Nazareth in Galilee to Judea, to the city of David called Bethlehem, because he was descended from the house and family of David. He went to be registered with Mary, to whom he was engaged and who was expecting a child. While they were there, the time came for her to deliver her child. And she gave birth to her firstborn son and wrapped him in bands of cloth, and laid him in a manger, because there was no place for them in the inn.

In that region there were shepherds living in the fields, keeping watch over their flock by night. Then an angel of the Lord stood before them, and the glory of the Lord shone around them, and they were terrified. But the angel said to them, "Do not be afraid; for see—I am bringing you good news of great joy for all the people: to you is born this day in the city of David a Savior, who is the Messiah, the Lord. This will be a sign for you: you will find a child wrapped in bands of cloth and lying in a manger." And suddenly there was with the angel a multitude of the heavenly host, praising God and saying, "Glory to God in the highest heaven, and on earth peace among those whom he favors!" (Luke 2:1–14—Gospel for Christmas Mass During the Night)

Christmas is the festival of gifts and lights. Parents give gifts to their children; spouses and friends exchange gifts with each other. We write letters and Christmas cards, wishing others peace and happiness in the soon-to-arrive new year. Lights in streets and city centers, in churches and houses, are reflected in our hearts to make the sometimes gray routine of our lives lighter and brighter.

For many people, including many who are not church-goers, Christmas represents a longing and a dream for another world of peace, joy, and friendship.

For Christians, Christmas is more than a longing or dream. It is an unexpected and wonderful reality. The word of the angel to the shepherds in the fields of Bethlehem makes this reality clear: "I am bringing you good news of great joy for all the people: to you is born this day in the city of David a Savior, who is the Messiah, the Lord."

In the best known of all the Christmas carols, "Silent Night," we sing: "Christ the Savior is born." He is the light shining in an otherwise often dark world and brightening our hearts with a new radiance. With him the longing for and human dream of a new beginning has been fulfilled in a wonderful way. In the smiling child in the manger something of the splendor of heavenly glory shines forth.

The many beautiful Christmas carols, familiar to us from childhood, are not only mood-lifting songs. They remind us: this is truth, reality; you are not dreaming. The miracle has happened. Just as the prophet Isaiah predicted, a rose has indeed sprung up.[1] A small shoot has sprung forth from what was believed to be a dead stump. In a way that no one ever could have expected, a bloom has appeared on this stump, "amid the cold of winter, when half spent was the night."

"Christ the Savior is born." God has not abandoned us in this dark world; God has come to us, become one of us, not in the palaces of the rich and powerful, but in the poverty of the manger among poor and simple shepherds in their fields.

God wanted to fill the ordinary lives of ordinary people with his presence and glory. Let no one say that this is a fairy tale or a myth, just like those found throughout world literature. No fairy tale invents such hard realities as the stable, the flight to Egypt, thirty silent and hidden years in Nazareth and, in the end, the gallows, the cross. This comes from real life—as the prayer over the gifts from the Christmas *Mass During the Night* has it: "O Lord, we pray that through this most holy exchange, we may be found in the likeness of Christ, in whom our nature is united to yours."[2] This prayer interprets for us what has happened at Christmas. It speaks of a "most holy exchange." God's Son became like us; he took on our meager human nature so that we can share in his divine nature.

---

1. Kasper is referring to Isaiah, chapter 11, verse 1, which inspired the German Christmas carol, *Es ist ein Ros entsprungen*. The usual English translation of this carol, "Lo, How a Rose E'er Blooming," does not quite catch Kasper's point—namely, that this prophecy has come to pass; it is reality.

2. Catholic Mass texts cited in this volume are taken from: *The Roman Missal: renewed by decree of the most holy Second Ecumenical Council of the Vatican, promulgated by authority of Pope Paul VI and revised at the direction of Pope John Paul II* (Collegeville, MN: Liturgical Press, 2011), 172.

So Christmas is no outer revolution, no externally imposed overthrowing of our nature. Christmas wants to take hold of our hearts and transform them. Christ, the Savior, must be born again in our hearts, in order to make us inwardly joyful and rich, so that we may join our own voices in gratitude with the beautiful Christmas carols that speak of joy and happiness:

> Good Christian men, rejoice
> With heart, and soul, and voice.[3]

But then the peace and joy of Christmas should also stream outward into the world. Christmas should be a day of presents, peace, and joy. And Christmas should be a day we spend not only in the trusted circle of family and friends. It should also be a day on which we think of the many who, like Mary and her child, are homeless, of the many who are lonely even this day, of the many who are on the run, and of the many who suffer because of their Christian faith or who suffer wrong and violence for whatever reason.

It is for us to carry the light of this holy night, to carry the message that "Christ, the Savior, is born" to those who have not yet heard it or who cannot yet believe it. Through us, they should encounter at least a warming ray of joy and light. The joy which the angel announced to the shepherds should, through our humanity and compassion, be shared with all peoples.

---

3. Again, this common English translation of a Latin and German carol of the Middle Ages does not quite get at the meaning of the original: *In dulci jubilo*, "in sweet rejoicing."

The Power of
Christmas Songs

And suddenly there was with the angel a multitude of the heavenly host, praising God and saying:

> "Glory to God in the highest heaven,
> and on earth peace among those whom he favors!"

When the angels had left them and gone into heaven, the shepherds said to one another, "Let us go now to Bethlehem and see this thing that has taken place, which the Lord has made known to us." So they went with haste and found Mary and Joseph, and the child lying in the manger. When they saw this, they made known what had been told them about this child; and all who heard it were amazed at what the shepherds told them. But Mary treasured all these words and pondered them in her heart. The shepherds returned, glorifying and praising God for all they had heard and seen, as it had been told them. (Luke 2:13–20—Gospel for Christmas Mass at Dawn)

In reading the infancy narratives in Luke's Gospel, we see how frequently the text speaks about singing. Already before his birth we hear about songs: for example, we hear of the *Magnificat* (Luke 1:46–55), the hymn of praise sung by the Virgin Mary during her visit to her cousin Elizabeth:

> My soul magnifies the Lord,
> and my spirit rejoices in God my Savior,
> for he has looked with favor on
> the lowliness of his servant.
> Surely, from now on all generations
> will call me blessed;
> for the Mighty One has done great things for me,
> and holy is his name.
> His mercy is for those who fear him
> from generation to generation.
> He has shown strength with his arm;
> he has scattered the proud in the
> thoughts of their hearts.
> He has brought down the
> powerful from their thrones,
> and lifted up the lowly;
> he has filled the hungry with good things,
> and sent the rich away empty.
> He has helped his servant Israel,
> in remembrance of his mercy,
> according to the promise he made
> to our ancestors,
> to Abraham and his descendants forever.

Later, Luke's Gospel reports the *Benedictus* (Luke 1:68–79), the hymn of praise of the priest Zechariah:

Blessed be the Lord God of Israel,
for he has looked favorably on his people
and redeemed them.
He has raised up a mighty savior for us
in the house of his servant David,
as he spoke through the mouth
of his holy prophets from of old,
that we would be saved from
our enemies and from the
hand of all who hate us.
Thus he has shown the mercy
promised to our ancestors,
and has remembered his holy covenant,
the oath that he swore to our ancestor Abraham,
to grant us, that we, being rescued
from the hands of our enemies,
might serve him without fear,
in holiness and righteousness
before him all our days.
And you, child, will be called the
prophet of the Most High;
for you will go before the Lord
to prepare his ways,
to give knowledge of salvation to his people
by the forgiveness of their sins.
By the tender mercy of our God,
the dawn from on high will break upon us,
to give light to those who sit in
darkness and in the shadow of death,
to guide our feet into the way of peace.

Then, in the Christmas story itself, Luke tells of the hymn of praise of the angel, the *Gloria* (Luke 2:14), proclaimed to the shepherds in the fields of Bethlehem:

> Glory to God in the highest heaven,
> and on earth peace among those whom he favors!

It is said of the shepherds that they went to the manger and praised God. As we read further, we hear of the song of praise of the aged Simeon and of the prophet Anna. We read the *Nunc dimittis* of Simeon (Luke 2:29–32):

> Master, now you are dismissing your servant in
>   peace,
> according to your word;
> for my eyes have seen your salvation,
> which you have prepared in the presence of all
>   peoples,
> a light for revelation to the Gentiles
> and for glory to your people Israel.

Christmas, especially as we celebrate it in Germany, is a time of song and of singing.

And we Germans have a great wealth of beautiful Christmas carols that, translated into many languages, are now sung all over the world.

At Christmas, we Christians have every reason to sing. For the good news of Christmas announces: "Christ, the Savior, is born!" God has not abandoned us. God does not leave us simply to chance or to fate. God has come down from heaven and become human. God wanted to be with us as one of us, sharing our life, with all that is good and beautiful in it, but also in its darkness and sadness. God took suffering and death upon himself.

God became fully human so that we can be with God in all the situations of our life. God shared our life so that we could come to share God's life, already now on earth and forever in heaven.

Therefore singing is part of our praise of God. But it is equally true the other way around: our praise of God should be in song. For singing is only possible for one with a good and happy heart; for one who knows: whatever happens, I am safe; God loves me and all people, and wants goodness for all of us. Without such faith, the human heart easily becomes heavy. Then human beings no longer see a way out; then, in the face of the world's condition, in the face of all that is wrong and evil and unjust in the world, they can almost fall into despair or into complaining and aimless criticism.

Faith in God, faith that God exists and is with us, can give us courage, confidence, and hope; and, despite everything, it can lead us to sing and make music. The biblical songs of praise teach us that whoever sings does not only suppress or forget his suffering but conquers it.

"Christ, the Savior, is born" means that neither blind accident, nor money, nor power, nor prestige finally determines our life. Our life belongs to God. We are lifted up by God, held and supported; we are accompanied and led by God, nourished by God's Word and filled inwardly by baptism and the other sacraments. This is our reason for giving thanks, for praising, for singing.

Through our singing, we raise ourselves above the everyday and proclaim: Our great God, it is good that you exist, that in Jesus you became human, that you have given our lives a purpose, a direction, and a great hope. We rejoice in this, and so we thank you. On account of all this, we praise you. Because of it, we sing. Whoever thus sings, prays twice.

Through our joyful singing, we want to be known as Christians; we want to give witness, and through our singing to pass on the good news to others. Today many no longer know of the gospel, or they no longer understand it. But our singing can attract them; it can go to their hearts and perhaps convey a ray of the light and joy that the Christmas message has kindled in our own hearts.

There is a famous example of this. Before his baptism, St. Augustine, one of the greatest theologians in the history of the church, led a rather dissolute life for a long time in Rome. But he was a serious person and searched for more; he wanted to make progress. So he tried one philosophy of life after another. But nothing totally satisfied him. Then he came into the cathedral in Milan, where the great Bishop Ambrose was preaching, and he heard singing. In his autobiography, the *Confessions*, as he himself titled it, he thanked God and wrote:

> How I wept during your hymns and songs! I was deeply moved by the music of the sweet chants of your Church. The sounds flowed into my ears and the truth was distilled into my heart. This caused the feelings of devotion to overflow. Tears ran, and it was good for me to have that experience.[1]

Through music, God penetrated his heart and opened him to the truth expressed in the sung text. For him music was thus a form of evangelization leading to his conversion and baptism. This is how he first became the great theologian, bishop, and church father whose writings we read to this day.

What will the time ahead, the new year, bring us? Of course, as human beings we are not able to answer this question. But as

---

1. St, Augustine, *Confessions*, Book IX: 6. The English translation of *The Confessions* cited here is *St. Augustine Confessions*, a new translation by Henry Chadwick (New York: Oxford University Press, 1991), 164.

Christians we know one thing: "Christ, the Savior, is born," and he alone is the savior. Only in him will we find salvation, healing, peace, and justice. Even now, he can be orientation, light, and strength for every chapter of our life. Our ancestors lived from this faith, and it is my firm conviction that no one can give us anything better along our own way. As Christians, we can and must orient ourselves on Christ; we can rely on him. Then nothing will lead us astray. We must place him at the beginning of each new start in our lives, and we must pass on his message to others: in what we say with words, even more in what we do and what we live, and, of course, also in our singing.

We Christians are not just some small group, not just a scattered handful of people; rather, if we all acted together as a large human chorus, we could give direction to the future. The future belongs to Jesus Christ. He *is* the future, and he is our hope.

Who We Are and Who We Can Be

In the beginning was the Word, and the Word was with God, and the Word was God. He was in the beginning with God. All things came into being through him, and without him not one thing came into being. What has come into being in him was life, and the life was the light of all people. The light shines in the darkness, and the darkness did not overcome it.

The true light, which enlightens everyone, was coming into the world. He was in the world and the world came into being through him; yet the world did not know him. He came to what was his own, and his own people did not accept him. But to all who received him, who believed in his name, he gave power to become children of God, who were born, not of blood or of the will of the flesh or of the will of man, but of God. And the Word became flesh and lived among us, and we have seen his glory, the glory as of a father's only son, full of grace and truth. (John 1:1–5, 9–14—Gospel for Christmas Mass During the Day)

"The Word became flesh." God became a human being: that is the message of Christmas. In the eleventh century, Anselm, a monk living in England, asked: "Why did God become a human being?" He wrote a famous book whose title is that very question: *Cur Deus Homo?* Why did God become human? His response was this: sin is so great, so powerful in our world, that only God could remedy it; only God is great and powerful enough to bring us healing and redemption.

That message is especially relevant in our day. Often enough we have the impression that there is no real progress any longer, in either great or small matters. An outer and inner paralysis, with resignation and fear, seems to be spreading. Great hopes for the future have vanished. Each day we read about war, injustice, and violence; we hear of marriages breaking down and of hunger, sickness, and despair. Some extremists think they can cut the Gordian knot by force.[1] But any sensible person knows that this only makes everything worse.

So, where is the way out? How can we make progress? The message of Christmas declares that our situation is difficult, but not so difficult that there is no way out. God has not let us down. For our sake and for our salvation, God came down from heaven and became human. And so the message of the angel to the shepherds in the fields of Bethlehem: "Do not be afraid" (Luke 2:10). Have no fear, summon up hope, take courage, and have faith! The star of Bethlehem shines on each one of you.

"The Word became flesh." God became a human being. This tells us who God is. The number of committed and absolute atheists is not large. But a very high percentage of human beings,

---

1. In Greek mythology, Alexander the Great is said to have tried to untie the knot which held a city's treasure. When he could not do so, he sliced the knot in half with a stroke of his sword.

even of Christians, have only a pale sense of God. Earlier many thought of God as a punishing God, whom one had to fear; today, for many people, God is completely distant, some higher being perhaps, but one who does not care for us and for whom we need take little care.

Yet the God who reveals himself to us at Christmas is not this nameless God, but a personal God who has a heart for human beings, whose heart has mercy on us, whose heart is turned inside out in response to our human suffering. He is a God who in Jesus Christ runs after us, who himself became human to experience in his own body all the distress, all the pain and suffering, violence, abandonment, and loneliness, all the helplessness of a small child, the loss of home and country of young parents, the disloyalty of friends, and the hatred of opponents. He is a God of human beings. Someone even put it this way: God is downright crazy about us human beings. God is in love with us. As the Christmas gospel puts it, God showers us with "grace upon grace."

This is a completely unimaginable message, one that no human brain or even a sophisticated computer could construct. In the face of this mystery of love, we can only—like the shepherds on that holy night—kneel in adoration. Again today we must learn this attitude of wonder and adoration; we must learn to say, consciously and simply, "thank you" for so much love and for the joy of Christmas.

In the incarnation of his Son, God not only tells us who he is; God also tells us who we are as human beings. And we need that too in our day, for many have lost their way. They no longer know why and for what purpose they are here. They feel worthless. Over the last century, the value and dignity of persons was often left by the wayside. There has been murder right from the very beginning, since Cain and Abel. But has there ever before been such terrible world wars, such awful weapons of mass destruction, and such brutal, contemptuous terrorism? Just how banal our understanding of humanity often is comes through when, in the face of injustice, unkindness, faithlessness, vanity, lies, and many other things, we say simply, "That's only human." On the contrary, must we not say that loyalty, decency, fairness, justice, and mercy are the real measure of our humanity and the true character of an authentically human culture?

In the incarnation, God has given a clear and final response to the question: What is a human being? The response rings out that the human being, every human being, is a being deserving both mercy and love. We need mercy because our own strength is unable to free us from our distress and our misery. In our misery, we rely on God's mercy. Our greatness is that we—every single one of us—are creatures deserving of love; we are so deserving of love that God himself became a human being. God wanted to be very close to us. And so every human being is of infinite value, completely independent of whether she is a native or a foreigner, healthy or ill, or old and disabled—completely independent of whether he is rich or poor. For God, every human being is worthy of love; every single one is infinitely valuable. God wanted to become a human being, so that we could share in his divine life.

Are we always conscious of this dignity of ours? Are we merciful human beings, in the way that God is merciful? Do we show mercy to others, or are we indifferent in the face of others' suffering? Have our interpersonal relationships become rather cold? Does not the human temperature of our world often threaten to fall below freezing? Christmas reveals a new culture of true humanity and human solidarity.

God shares in the weakness of our humanity in order to give us a share in God's own divine life. Whoever has been in Bethlehem and visited the Church of the Nativity knows that one can only enter through a very low doorway; one must stoop down in order to enter. To me, that seems symbolic of God making himself small as he came into this world. And so we must not puff ourselves up. We must humble ourselves if we want to approach the child in the manger, and we must bow down before our fellow human beings. We are greatest when we kneel down and pray.

And so why did God become a human being? God wanted to show both who he is and who we are. God did not only want to show it, but to model and live it bodily. God wanted to bring the warmth of divine love into our world that had turned tired and cold. God wanted to break the ice between himself and us, and between us and our fellow human beings. Christmas is the triumph of grace, compassion, and love. They shine forth as light from the face of the child in the manger.

PART FOUR

FOLLOWING THE CHRISTMAS STAR— EPIPHANY, BAPTISM OF THE LORD, AND BEYOND

The Path of Worship

In the time of King Herod, after Jesus was born in Bethlehem of Judea, wise men from the East came to Jerusalem, asking, "Where is the child who has been born king of the Jews? For we observed his star at its rising, and have come to pay him homage." When King Herod heard this, he was frightened, and all Jerusalem with him; and calling together all the chief priests and scribes of the people, he inquired of them where the Messiah was to be born. They told him, "In Bethlehem of Judea; for so it has been written by the prophet:

> 'And you, Bethlehem, in the land of Judah,
> are by no means least among the rulers of Judah;
> for from you shall come a ruler
> who is to shepherd my people Israel.'"

Then Herod secretly called for the wise men and learned from them the exact time when the star had appeared. Then he sent them to Bethlehem, saying, "Go and search diligently for the child, and when you have found him, bring me word so that I may also go and pay him homage." When they had heard the king, they set out; and there, ahead of them, went the star that they had seen at its rising, until it stopped over the place where the child was. When they saw that the star had stopped, they were overwhelmed with joy. On entering the house, they saw the child with Mary his mother; and they knelt down and paid him homage. Then, opening their treasure chests, they offered him gifts of gold, frankincense, and myrrh. And having been warned in a dream not to return to Herod, they left for their own country by another road. (Matt 2:1–12—Gospel of the Feast of the Epiphany of the Lord)

One of the infancy narratives in Matthew's Gospel is well known to us as the story of the Three Kings. In truth, they were no kings; rather, these persons were wise and learned men of their time—which means that, like all who are truly learned, they were questioning and searching persons. They observed the course and alignment of the stars. But they were not only concerned with how the stars pursued their course across the night sky; they were also interested in the fate of persons here on earth. They saw the injustice, violence, hatred, egoism, and hypocrisy that were at work in the world then as in all times, including ours now. They saw immense suffering in the world, very much in the way that our contemporary *Sternsinger* remind us of those realities today with their singing and collections.[1] The wise men knew that situations

1. A website for Americans who want to understand German customs explains the contemporary tradition of the *Sternsinger*: "Every year between Christmas and Epiphany, hundreds of thousands of German kids travel from house to house singing carols and collecting money for good causes. These kids are known as *Sternsinger* ('star singers'), and their efforts are part of a Catholic initiative that has been ongoing since 1959. Between December 25 and January 6, these kids dress up in colorful robes, wear gold crowns and carry a star. They represent the three Wise Men (Magi). When they arrive at a Catholic house, they sing carols and bless the house by writing an inscription over the door with a stick

of injustice must not be allowed to continue on and on. The search and longing for the Messiah, a Savior, burnt in the hearts of these three wise men.

But they were wise enough to know this: a human being, however wise and powerful, cannot bring salvation; we human beings cannot accomplish this, we cannot make it happen. In the past, whenever human beings have cast themselves as messiahs, it has gone very badly wrong and only brought on greater disasters. The cry *"Heil Hitler!"* brought horrors to Germany and to the world. Only God can bring salvation.[2] And, so, these three wise men waited and hoped; and then one day they believed they saw a sign in the heavens.

These three wise men were Gentiles, not orthodox believers of their day. But such people also have something to teach us. In recent years, in many trips to other continents, I have often encountered people of other cultures who have shaken their heads about us clever Europeans and said to me, It just makes no sense that there can be a culture without God! And, in fact, as far as we can look back in human history, there never has been a culture without God. Wherever it has been tried—for example, in the mandated state atheism of communist systems—we know only too well how it has turned out. Our contemporary difficulties in Europe stem less from the so-called "new atheism" movement than from the indifference and shallowness that is content with superficiality and with whatever the current fashion is. But the three wise men of the gospel tell us, on the contrary: we should be questioning, seeking, and hoping human beings, not people who live our lives in indifference and dullness. We should be people who follow a star, who have ideals, who search and ask about

---

of chalk. At the same time, these kids ask for donations for various charities and causes." See: http://www.germany.info/Vertretung/usa/en/__pr/GIC/TWIG__WoW/2016/01-Sternsinger.html.

2. The word for *salvation* in German is *Heil*. Kasper is underlining that Hitler posed as a human messiah.

---

the mystery that we name God. *Quaerere Deum*, seek God[3]: This is what distinguishes us as human beings, this is the measure of human greatness and dignity. Once we no longer do this, then, in the words of Karl Rahner, we will have "regressed to the level of a clever animal."[4]

The three wise men of Matthew's Gospel were questioning and searching persons. But they were not only that. As they saw the sign in the heavens, they set out. They left everything behind and were not afraid of the struggles of a long journey. They set out on the path on their own two feet.

Setting out: we encounter this idea again and again in the Bible. Abraham, our father in faith, set out in response to the call of God. The people of Israel set out and left Egypt, and they were led toward the Promised Land. The first disciples of Jesus set out: Jesus called them, and they followed him. And we know that many great saints did this same thing: they set out and began a new life. And from the great teachers of theology and spirituality, we also know that sloth, idleness, rigidity—however we name it—is among the most fundamental of sins.

And isn't that precisely the temptation we face? We are tempted to live as everyone lives, to say what everyone says, to do what everyone does, and to behave as everyone does. But that is not at all the way of Jesus. He said, Repent! Change the direction of your life! Christians must have the courage to live, to judge, and to act in a way that is worthy of the gospel, and thus in many ways

---

3. St. Benedict (AD 480–547) says in his "rule" that *Quaerere Deum* is the basic task of all monks.

4   See Rahner's "Meditation on the Word 'God,'" in *Foundations of Christian Faith: An Introduction to the Idea of Christianity*, trans. William V. Dych (New York: Crossroad, 1978), 58.

---

to live differently, judge differently, and act differently than seems culturally and politically convenient.

The three wise men were questioning and searching persons, and they dared to set out. And when they encountered that "old fox" Herod (Luke 13:32), they experienced the opposition that rises up against goodness and the coming of God. Herod's aim was to preserve his power and wealth; he wasn't interested in any messiah. And so he responded, not in a squeamish way, but very brutally—as demonstrated by the slaughter of the innocents. He tried to interrogate the three wise men, to manipulate them, to use them for his own selfish goals. But they did not allow themselves to be hoodwinked or to be used. They would not let themselves be played for fools. They went their own way.

Christians must always reckon with resistance. The Second Vatican Council said that the church goes its way in history encountering afflictions and persecutions.[5] That did not only apply to the persecution of Christians under the Emperor Nero, or under Hitler and Stalin; it is still happening today. In our own day, we see that Christians are among the most persecuted and oppressed groups in many parts of the world. But let us not delude ourselves: even in western societies many would like, if not to drive out Christianity, at least to marginalize it and banish its symbols from public life. One need not at all be a prophet to see that the situation of the church will become harder. The wise men of the gospel are our teachers: We should follow our own star; we

---

5. Kasper seems to be referring to a text in paragraph nine of Vatican II's *Dogmatic Constitution on the Church Lumen Gentium*: "The Church is destined to extend to all regions of the earth and so enters into the history of humanity. Moving forward through trial and tribulation, the Church is strengthened by the power of God's grace." The English translation is from Austin Flannery, ed., *Vatican Council II: The Basic Sixteen Documents, A Completely Revised Translation in Inclusive Language* (Northport, NY: Costello Publishing Company, 1996).

should follow the voice of our conscience, and ask ourselves the most essential questions! We should dedicate ourselves to what is essential! So, let us set out on the way, and we will find God. Precisely now, we need dedicated and courageous Christians who do not bend to the pressures of public opinion.

The three wise men were questioning people, people on the move, courageous witnesses. But the most important is yet to come. When the three wise men arrived at their destination, they fell down and worshipped the child in the manger as the Messiah, the Son of God come into the world, the only one able to bring us salvation and life.

The star that the wise men followed led them neither to a palace of the rich and powerful nor to an academy of scholars, but to a child. These three were truly wise human beings, for they understood that God does not normally come to us in extraordinary, unusual, extravagant, adventurous, sensational ways—or in spectacular events. Certainly, we may not rule out extraordinary experiences; occasionally God gives us such signs. But they are not to be expected. In fact, the great saints were always reticent, even highly critical about supposedly miraculous events. What is truly wonderful is not found in exceptional occurrences. What is truly wonderful is that the extraordinary happens right in the middle of everyday, quite ordinary life. God does not produce spectacles or shows. God is—if one may put it this way—discreet, just as real human love is never intrusive but always discreet. This is how God is. God comes down to us; God wants to be visible and present in our midst, in the middle of the everyday life of the world.

The three wise men were overwhelmed by this miracle of great love. God became a human being in Jesus Christ—a human being like you and me, with only our sin excluded.

God was born, was a little child, was troubled by hunger

and thirst, experienced joy and friendship, endured suffering and then died.

In adoring the child, the wise men make clear what matters, what lasts and what is important. Here is the ultimate measure and criterion by which we are to decide and judge: Jesus Christ. In him the invisible and hidden God, who dwells in unapproachable light and who is an impenetrable and inaccessible mystery for us human beings, has become visible. In Jesus Christ, God has taken on flesh and has become one of us. And in this way, he has helped us to distinguish between the true God and false idols. Whoever looks to him and listens to him does not go astray. In regard to himself, Jesus Christ said that whoever sees him also sees the Father. He is the way, the truth, and the life (John 14:6).

At Christmas, God, before whom we kneel in adoration, revealed definitively that he is no tyrant or dictator; rather, God is pure love for us and all people. The church fathers tell us again and again that God became a human being so that we can be divinized and filled with divine life, already here on earth and fully in eternity—where we will be with God forever and God will give us eternal life.

Thus, truth, as we Christians understand it, is no abstract principle, no code of doctrines, or of dos and don'ts. Truth is not a rigid and static matter. Truth is not something one finds between the two covers of a book. Truth is a person; it is Jesus Christ in person. He tells us who God is and what God is like; and he likewise tells us who we are and what we should be like as human beings; he shows us how we can live life in its fullness and find true happiness in life.

Today, many no longer know what they should do with their lives, what they need to leave behind, where they are coming from, and where they are going. What is wonderful and beautiful about Christianity is that in Jesus Christ we have a tangible standard and point of orientation, the good shepherd and our leader in life, to whom we can absolutely entrust ourselves.

The three wise men were right in bowing down before the only thing in the world before which it makes sense to bow down. There is nowhere else that we should genuflect. But when we genuflect before Jesus, we lose absolutely nothing of our human dignity; we leave absolutely nothing of our human wisdom and insight behind. To bow down before Jesus is not to make oneself small; on the contrary, in so doing a human being experiences her true greatness or his true calling. The posture of worship does not make us small, but it does save us from pretension. It says to us: here is one who is greater than all powers of the world.

This is how it was for the three wise men. As they came to the child and his mother, they fell to their knees and worshipped the child. Before this God who acts so differently than most people have ever imagined, one can only fall to one's knees. Here worship is a sign of grateful wonder and of love reciprocated. The wise men brought gold, frankincense, and myrrh. They offered themselves as a sign of their reciprocated love.

In our own day, we must learn again to worship in this way. We must learn to be silent and become aware that there is someone greater, one whose love embraces each and every one of us, and whose infinite love sustains (and at times suffers) us, who means well with us, accepts us, and forgives us again and again. It is enough, then, to say, "I thank you that you exist, that you are there for me. And I love you, too," and then consciously to genuflect, not as an afterthought, not because it is customary, but because this is what we owe to the great God before whom we can humble ourselves without becoming small.

The gospel story of the three wise men teaches us that Christmas ought not be reduced to a feeling, a mood. Let Christmas lead us to worship. For it says to us, God is here.

To Whom the Future Belongs

Blessed be the God and Father of our Lord Jesus Christ, who has blessed us in Christ with every spiritual blessing in the heavenly places, just as he chose us in Christ before the foundation of the world to be holy and blameless before him in love. He destined us for adoption as his children through Jesus Christ, according to the good pleasure of his will, to the praise of his glorious grace that he freely bestowed on us in the Beloved. In him we have redemption through his blood, the forgiveness of our trespasses, according to the riches of his grace that he lavished on us. With all wisdom and insight he has made known to us the mystery of his will, according to his good pleasure that he set forth in Christ, as a plan for the fullness of time, to gather up all things in him, things in heaven and things on earth. In Christ we have also obtained an inheritance, having been destined according to the purpose of him who accomplishes all things according to his counsel and will, so that we, who were the first to set our hope on Christ, might live for the praise of his glory. In him you also, when you had heard the word of truth, the gospel of your salvation, and had believed in him, were marked with the seal of the promised Holy Spirit; this is the pledge of our inheritance toward redemption as God's own people, to the praise of his glory (Eph 1:3–14—the second reading for Mass on the Second Sunday after Christmas[1]).

It cannot always be Christmas, but we may absolutely wish that some of the peace and joy of this feast remain with us into the new year. This hymn from the Letter to the Ephesians invites us to take a look back to what we actually celebrated at Christmas, and then to look ahead to what remains of Christmas in our everyday life in the new year.

   The hymn itself is the outcome of a retrospective look back, the outcome of long and deep reflection on the events described in a vividly concrete and moving way in the Gospel of Luke: the birth in the manger at Bethlehem, the message and song of the angels, and the adoration of the shepherds.

   Through thoughtful and prayerful reflection, it dawned on the author of Ephesians just how great a thing happened in those events. For him this was no sweet, romantic indulgence, some pious sentiment, a family celebration with gifts and pleasantries, and certainly not just a few days of good food and sleeping in. Of course, all of that has its place, and all of us need such festivities from time to time. Nothing should be said against such a human sense of joy at Christmas.

   But the reflection of the Ephesians hymn goes much deeper. The beginnings of salvation lead back not only to the time of the Emperor Augustus, but back to the primordial origins of the

---

1. "The Second Sunday after Christmas" is celebrated in places where Epiphany occurs on January 6. But dioceses may decide to celebrate Epiphany on the second Sunday after Christmas. Since most dioceses in the United States do this, American Catholics usually do not hear the readings for the "Second Sunday after Christmas."

world and of time, even back into eternity. God chose us before the very beginning. God thought of every single one of us and of all peoples, intending to save us through this child in the manger, to make us his sons and daughters in the image of this child, to be light and life for our own journey, and to shower us with grace upon grace. What is revealed to us in the child in the manger, as in the crucified one on Golgotha, is the deepest mystery of our whole life and of the whole world. None of us is here by accident, the result of the winds of fate and chance. We have been willed and loved from all eternity; we are held and supported.

Even more: we are called to something higher. The fathers of the church said it clearly and unequivocally. God became a human being so that we could become divine, filled with the life of God. Pope St. Leo the Great put it this way: "Christian, remember your dignity, and be aware that you share in God's own nature."[2]

O, human being, accept the mystery that you are! Do not think too small about yourself, and do not live beneath yourself. Do not settle for small-mindedness, accepting a life of small and narrow pleasures. Do not become a small joyless workaholic and certainly no petty fault-finder and quibbler, one who sits passively and watches until he finds something to criticize. Guard and keep something of the joy and peace of Christmas in your heart. You have every reason to do so as a Christian. You have been chosen from all eternity for happiness in communion with God.

And so we already live in anticipation of what we shall be. Of course, none of us knows what the new year will bring. And that is a good thing. For if we knew of all our difficulties in advance, they would only become more difficult. The anticipation would spoil even the good days to come. And, vice versa, if we knew in advance of all the good and beautiful things that may yet

---

2. Pope St. Leo the Great, Sermon XXI: 3. This is Kasper's second reference to this text that inspires the title of this volume: see the note in Kasper's foreword to this book for a reference to an English translation of the sermon.

come, leaving no joyful surprises, they would become only half so good.

The Ephesians hymn tells us something different in advance, not about tomorrow or the day after. It tells us that the future began at Christmas, and now everything is moving toward the fulfillment of what began there. Everything in heaven and on earth, everything in the cosmos, will be gathered together and transfigured in Christ. The radiance of Christmas should shine on all things. For the future belongs to the child in the manger. Jesus Christ is the Alpha and the Omega, the beginning and the end, the origin and destiny of all that is. We do not know what tomorrow and the next day will bring, but as Christians we know that everything runs toward Jesus Christ and flows and opens out into God's kingdom and God's eternity.

Some may consider us Christians to be dreamers and odd-balls, thinking of us as chasing after a utopia and a deceptive mirage. But where is their hope? Do they have something better to offer? They think and say, "Let us eat and drink, for tomorrow we die. Let's enjoy life to its fullest while we can."[3] And the state of our contemporary world seems to prove them right. Many think that Christianity and Christians will simply decline; we might as well forget all that. And so many persons do forget it. Even so-called Catholic areas have become more worldly and de-Christianized. But has this made us happier?

In any case, the Holy Spirit has always been good for surprises, and so also in our day. (Just a short while ago, who could have imagined the pontificate of Pope Francis? And, in the meanwhile, a jolt has passed through the church.) It all depends on whether we will allow ourselves to be surprised by the Spirit, whether we are ready to break out from our prejudices and narrow schemes, whether we will open ourselves to rediscover the

---

3. Both the prophet Isaiah (22:13) and Paul, in his First Letter to the Corinthians (15:32), use a form of this expression to say that lack of faith brings fatalism.

relevance of the Christmas message. No one has anything better to offer us.

An instructive story from Greek mythology tells of the princess Ariadne, who gave Theseus a ball of thread to help him find his way through a maze; as he entered the maze, Theseus could unwind the thread and, then, with its help, find his way back to the entrance of the maze. And so we speak proverbially about an Ariadne's thread: even today such threads are used by spelunkers going into caves and by deep-sea divers. But it is not only they who need this; we too need such a thread to keep from becoming lost in the maze of our own lives and instead find our way.

Jesus Christ is that thread. At Christmas he stepped out of eternity and down from heaven to be with us in the world. With his hand guiding us, we can make it; we can find our way to the ultimate goal of our lives. With him leading us, we can master the way back from the festivities of Christmas to our everyday lives, and then we can find our way in the midst of the demands of our lives. He is the light and the star that we follow, the way, the truth, and the life.

The Holy Exchange

The beginning of the good news of Jesus Christ, the Son of God. As it is written in the prophet Isaiah,

> "See, I am sending my messenger ahead of you,
> who will prepare your way;
> the voice of one crying out in the wilderness:
> 'Prepare the way of the Lord,
> make his paths straight,'"

John the baptizer appeared in the wilderness, proclaiming a baptism of repentance for the forgiveness of sins. He proclaimed, "The one who is more powerful than I is coming after me; I am not worthy to stoop down and untie the thong of his sandals. I have baptized you with water; but he will baptize you with the Holy Spirit."

In those days Jesus came from Nazareth of Galilee and was baptized by John in the Jordan. And just as he was coming up out of the water, he saw the heavens torn apart and the Spirit descending like a dove on him. And a voice came from heaven, "You are my Son, the Beloved; with you I am well pleased" (Mark 1:1–4, 7–11—Gospel for the Feast of the Baptism of the Lord, Lectionary Cycle B).

The gospel story of the baptism of Jesus summarizes the whole mystery of Christmas. In the Eastern Churches, it is read at Mass on the Feast of the Epiphany; in the Western Church, it is the gospel for the Feast of the Baptism of the Lord, the Sunday that closes the Christmas season.

In this way, the liturgical traditions make clear how the evangelist Mark understood the text.

He introduces the story of the baptism of Jesus with a striking statement: "The beginning of the good news of Jesus Christ, the Son of God" (Mark 1:1). "The beginning," *arché* in the Gospel's Greek text, is not a casual reference to the first sentence of Mark's Gospel, but is the foundation of everything else that follows. The story of Jesus' baptism is the prelude in which all the themes of the Gospel are already discernible, for the whole story is the Gospel of Jesus Christ the Son of God. In himself Jesus Christ sums up all the mysteries of faith; he is the beginning, middle, and end of all salvation history and of all reality.

But who is Jesus Christ? That is the foundational question. Already Jesus himself directed this question to his disciples, asking, "Who do people say that the Son of Man is?" (Matt 16:13). What do you think, what do you have to say about me? Indeed, what do we think and say and believe about him?

If we were to organize a survey in our day, we could respond to this foundational question now very much in the way that the disciples responded in their day: Some say this, and others say that. Some take him to be a good man, a kind of philanthropist, while others see him as a courageous social reformer and still others as an unappreciated religious genius or a prophet.

At this point, right at the beginning of the Gospel, the story of Jesus' baptism foils our survey. It does not deny that Jesus is any of these things. Of course, he was a good man; of course, he was a religious genius, if the term is properly understood; and, of course, he stood in the tradition of the prophets. But John the Baptist instructs us that he is more than that. He is more powerful than the Baptist who was the greatest of the prophets and who made a powerful impression on his contemporaries (Mark 13:32). He is greater than Jonah, and greater than Solomon (Matt 12:41–42).

He towers over all who came before him and over all whose coming was eagerly awaited. In him something new and greater has come. What the scriptures of Israel hoped for was not only at an earthly messiah, an earthly justice, an earthly paradise. The scriptures awaited the coming of the Spirit of God who would renew all things in a fundamental way from within; they awaited one who would baptize not only with water, but with the Holy Spirit.

For God alone can truly bring salvation. Only God can establish a new beginning and bring forth a new creation. Human beings can do what is humanly possible, but our soul longs for more. Only God is big enough to fulfill the vastness of the longings of the human heart.

The Old Testament awaited the coming of God himself. The story of Jesus' baptism makes use of three images that the Old Testament used to describe the coming of God.

The *first* image is of the opening of the heavens. As Mark's Gospel puts it, Jesus saw the opening of the heavens. In the view of Judaism at that time, the heavens, symbolizing direct access to God, were closed. It was like living through a foggy day cloaked in clouds, where one could barely see the hand in front of her face and could easily become disoriented while walking. Now, claims the Gospel, the horizon has cleared; we can find our way again, for the way ahead has been made clear. Therefore, the New Testament refers to Jesus as "light," as light of the world and light of life. As the great Nicene Creed puts is, he is "Light from Light." Only in his light can we perceive the true essence of things. We need such a light in our confused and fragmented situation.

The *second* image is of the Spirit descending upon Jesus like a dove. The dove reminds us of the end of the flood and Noah's release of a dove: its return with a green twig signals the end of the flood and testifies to the new peace between heaven and earth (Gen 8:8–11). The dove continues to be a symbol of peace up to our own time, as the promise of a renewed and reconciled world. But we human beings cannot "make" a definitive peace happen, a peace that overcomes all unjust social conditions. This peace must begin in the human heart; it requires a new, reconciled heart, a heart at peace with God.

Jesus comes as the one bearing God's Spirit who was promised by the prophet Isaiah, the one anointed by the Holy Spirit and born of that Spirit (Isa 1:2; Luke 1:32; 4:18; John 1:33; Acts 10:38). Jesus comes as the redeemer who can change human beings' hearts, heal our wounds, and reconcile all hurts that remain from past injustice.

Jesus comes as the light of life and as the breath of life. These two ideas are summarized in a *third* image or, better, in a third proclamation. A voice from the heavens says: "You are my Son, the Beloved; with you I am well pleased." These words from Psalm 2:7 are used to proclaim Jesus as the awaited kingly messiah, albeit in a way that goes far beyond the expectation of the Old Testament. He is the very Son of God, and has been so from all eternity (John 1:34; 8:58). He is the eternal self-communication of the love of God, who took on flesh in history, that is, who became a human being (John 1:14).

Before such proclamations, one simply falls silent and marvels. But the actual point of this gospel story comes next. The one who is God's Son from all eternity allows himself to be baptized by John the Baptist. Although he is without sin, he places himself in the midst of sinners in solidarity with all of us. John is frightened by the request and does not want to comply with it. But Jesus' response is clear: he wants to fulfill all righteousness (Matt 3:13–15). He himself receives the baptism of repentance from John as the representative of us all. He is God's servant suffering vicariously for us (Isa 1—4; 53:1–12). He is the Lamb of God who takes away the sin of the world (John 1:29). It happens through a holy exchange. He, the guiltless one takes the guilt of all of us upon himself, in order to free us from guilt. Here is how it is said in the *Third Preface for Christmas*:

> For through him the holy exchange that restores our life has shone forth today in splendor: when our frailty is assumed by your Word not only does human mortality receive unending honor but by this wondrous union we, too, are made eternal.[1]

In the Son, Jesus Christ, all of us should become sons and daughters of God: "But to all who received him, who believed in his name, he gave power to become children of God" (John 1:12). God wants to say to every single one of us: You are my son, my daughter. With you I am well pleased. I have taken you by the hand and will accompany and lead you. I love you.

In fact, all of that happened in our baptism. Since all of that has happened to us, we can join in with our whole hearts singing the hymn of the early church, picked up from the song of the angel at Christmas:

---

1. *The Roman Missal*, 542.

> Glory to God in the highest heaven,
> and on earth peace
> to people of good will.
> We praise you, we bless you,
> we adore you, we glorify you,
> we give you thanks for your great glory.

If we truly wish to bring Christmas into our daily lives, then let us allow the sweet song of the angels to resonate not only in our ears, but also and especially in our souls.

Index of Biblical Verses

About the Author

Walter Kasper (born in 1933) earned his doctorate in theology and, for decades, was professor of dogmatic theology. He was ordained a bishop in 1989 and served as Bishop of the German Diocese of Rottenburg-Stuttgart from 1989 to 1999. In 1999, Kasper was appointed secretary of the Pontifical Council for Promoting Christian Unity—and as such, president of the Pontifical Commission for Religious Relations with the Jews—and resigned from his post in Rottenburg-Stuttgart. He was elevated to cardinal in 2001 by Pope John Paul II and served as president of the Pontifical Council for Promoting Christian Unity from 2001 to 2010. He also served as a member of the Congregation for the Doctrine of the Faith and of the Congregation for the Oriental Churches.

Cardinal Kasper is the main author of the first volume of the German *Catholic Catechism for Adults* and chief editor of the third edition of the *Lexikon für Theologie und Kirche.* His collected works are being published by Herder Verlag in Germany and by Paulist Press in the United States. They are edited by George Augustine and Klaus Krämer. His book *Pope Francis' Revolution of Tenderness and Love: Theological and Pastoral Perspectives,* first published in Germany in 2015, has been translated into English (Paulist Press, 2015) and many other languages.